Who Was
Louis Armstrong?

Who Was
Louis Armstrong?

by Yona Zeldis McDonough

illustrated by John O'Brien

Penguin Workshop

For Jane O'Connor, editor extraordinaire—YZM

For Tess—JOB

PENGUIN WORKSHOP
An Imprint of Penguin Random House LLC, New York

Visit us online at www.penguinrandomhouse.com.

Library of Congress Control Number: 2003024471

ISBN 9780448433684   40 39 38 37

Contents

Who Was
Louis Armstrong?

Once, there was a poor Black boy who grew up in New Orleans in the early years of the twentieth century. His name was Louis Armstrong. But people called him Little Louie. To help his family, he did all kinds of jobs. He hunted for bits of brass and tinfoil that he sold to junk dealers. He peddled newspapers on the streets, and he ran errands for grown-ups.

Louis also formed a singing group with three of his friends. The boys stood on a corner and sang. People gave them money.

On New Year's Eve, when Little Louie was about twelve, he and his friends went out to sing. They had just finished a song called "My Brazilian Beauty" and were on their way home. One of his pals took out a cap gun and shot it into the air. He wanted to make noise, because it was New Year's Eve. Louie did, too. And he had a real gun. He took it out and pointed it up at the sky. *Bam! Bam! Bam!* A policeman heard the gunshots. Shooting a

gun was very dangerous. It was also against the law. The policeman took Louie down to the station, and the next day he was sent to a reform school. Reform schools were for boys who were too young to be sent to jail.

Years later, Louis Armstrong remembered that he thought his world was coming to an end then. As it turned out, going to the reform school saved his life. While he was in the school, he learned to play the cornet. He learned to play it so well that

CORNET

he grew up to become one of the greatest jazz musicians of all time. He composed dozens of songs that have become famous, and his music is still heard and loved today.

Chapter 1
A Rough and Tumble Start

Louis Armstrong was born in 1901 in a poor, Black section of New Orleans called Storyville. It was so dangerous that its nickname was the Battlefield. Many people carried guns or knives wherever they went. There was lots of crime.

Louis's mother, Mayann Armstrong, had to support her two children all by herself. Sometimes,

STORYVILLE

she worked as a maid. Sometimes, she went away for days at a time. Louis and his little sister Beatrice were often left with their grandmother. Her name was Josephine, and she had been enslaved. Now, she made a living washing and ironing clothes for white people. She gave Louis a nickel to pick up and deliver her wash loads. It made him feel rich.

Josephine was very strict. She made Louis go to school, to church, and to Sunday school. When he was bad, she swatted his behind with a branch. But later, Louis was grateful for her concern. She

wanted to keep him out of trouble because she cared about what happened to him.

It was not easy to be a young Black boy in the early 1900s. Though slavery had ended in 1865, many white people thought Black people were not as good as white people. Black people were often treated unfairly.

JIM CROW LAWS

SLAVERY ENDED IN 1865. ALL ENSLAVED BLACK PEOPLE BECAME FREE MEN AND WOMEN. BUT IN THE 1880S AND 1890S, NEW LAWS WERE PASSED IN THE SOUTH THAT RESTRICTED THE RIGHTS OF PEOPLE OF COLOR. THEY HAD TO SIT IN SEPARATE RAILROAD CARS, ATTEND SEPARATE SCHOOLS, USE SEPARATE PUBLIC REST-ROOMS AND WATER FOUNTAINS. PEOPLE OF COLOR COULDN'T EAT IN CERTAIN RESTAU-RANTS, STAY IN CERTAIN HOTELS, OR LIVE IN CERTAIN NEIGHBORHOODS. THEY WERE TREATED AS SECOND-CLASS CITIZENS.

THE LAWS WERE KNOWN AS JIM CROW LAWS. THE NAME CAME FROM A CHARACTER IN MINSTREL SHOWS, USUALLY PLAYED BY A WHITE MAN MADE UP TO APPEAR BLACK. THESE TERRIBLE LAWS REMAINED UNTIL THE 1950S AND 1960S.

Once, Louis got on a streetcar with his little sister Beatrice and a family friend who was babysitting them. There were lots of empty seats up front, so Louis sat down.

The babysitter told him to come back and sit with her and Beatrice. But Louis didn't want to. It was more fun to sit in front. He could see where the streetcar was headed. When he didn't move, she got up and dragged him to the back and forced him to sit with her. If she hadn't, all three of them could have been thrown off the bus or beaten up. Even arrested. Seats in the front were for white people only.

Another time, Louis and his friends were swimming in a local pond. One of the boys lost his bathing suit and the others were trying to help him find it. All of a sudden, a white man whose house was by the pond took his shotgun from its rack on the porch. He aimed it right at the boys.

"We were scared stiff," Louis later recalled.

Luckily, the white man didn't shoot. He put down the gun and laughed. He thought it was a big joke to scare the boys.

The neighborhood where Louis lived was poor and tough. He liked to play with older boys. They taught him to throw dice for money and to play cards. When he won, he ran home and gave the money to his mother. He didn't live with her all the time, but he always adored her. If anyone said anything bad about her, he wouldn't listen. Later, he said, "She held her head up at all times . . . . What she didn't have, she did without."

Louis always had a lot of nicknames. Back then, drinking water was kept in a bucket. A long-handled ladle, called a dipper, was used to pour the water from the bucket into a cup. Louis, like most kids, liked to drink straight from the dipper. He could drink a whole mouthful in one big gulp. So kids called him Dipper. They

also called him Gatemouth, or Gate. They even called him Satchelmouth because his wide, full mouth looked like an open suitcase, or satchel, as it used to be called.

When Louis was about seven, he got a job selling newspapers on street corners. Then he went to work for the Karnofskys. They were a Jewish family that had come from Russia. They had a wagon, which they drove around the city, buying and

selling rags, bottles, paper, and anything else people had to sell. The driver of the junk wagon blew on a long, tin horn to let people know the wagon was on their street. Sometimes, he let Louis blow the horn, too. Later, Louis said, "The kids . . . loved the sound of my tin horn."

Even then, Louis was interested in music. There was plenty of it, especially jazz, to hear in New Orleans. The bars and the dance halls all had live music. Even though he was too young to go into places like that, the music would drift out into the street, where Louis could stand and listen. Sometimes, a band would play on the street for a little while as a way of getting more customers to come inside. Louis had his favorite musicians. Joe Oliver was one. He played the cornet.

JAZZ: AMERICAN MUSIC

JAZZ IS A KIND OF MUSIC THAT GREW UP IN AND AROUND NEW ORLEANS, LOUISIANA. LATER, IT THRIVED IN CHICAGO AND NEW YORK CITY. JAZZ IS A MIXTURE OF DIFFERENT STYLES OF MUSIC AND TRADITIONS. WHEN AFRICANS WERE FORCED TO COME TO THIS COUNTRY AS SLAVES, THEY BROUGHT WITH THEM THEIR OWN WAYS OF MAKING MUSIC. THEY ALSO HEARD OTHER KINDS OF MUSIC: BRASS BANDS, GOSPEL MUSIC SUNG IN CHURCHES, SPANISH MUSIC. ALL THESE DIFFERENT KINDS OF MUSIC WERE BLENDED TOGETHER. THE RESULT WAS JAZZ.

JAZZ WAS A NEW AND ORIGINAL SOUND. IT WAS CREATED BY BLACK MUSICIANS AND FIRST PLAYED IN THE LATE 1890S. ORIGINALLY CALLED "JASS," THE NAME WAS LATER CHANGED TO JAZZ.

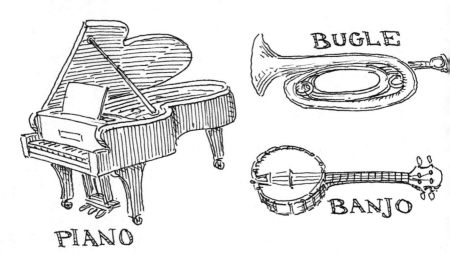

PIANO

BUGLE

BANJO

HERE ARE SOME IMPORTANT THINGS TO KNOW ABOUT JAZZ MUSIC:

- IMPROVISATION: JAZZ WAS NOT PLAYED JUST FROM WRITTEN NOTES. MANY JAZZ MUSICIANS COULD NOT EVEN READ MUSIC. INSTEAD, MUCH OF THE MUSIC WAS IMPROVISED, OR MADE UP, AS THE MUSICIANS WENT ALONG.

- MUSICAL NOTES THAT ARE "BENT" OR "SLURRED" ARE COMMON IN JAZZ. THESE NOTES ARE CALLED "BLUE NOTES" AND CAN SOUND SAD OR HAPPY OR ANGRY.

- IN JAZZ, THE RHYTHM OR BEAT COMES FROM DIFFERENT INSTRUMENTS IN THE BAND, NOT JUST THE DRUM. THE OTHER INSTRUMENTS IN A JAZZ BAND ARE THE CORNET, TRUMPET, VIOLIN, ALTO SAXOPHONE, SLIDE TROMBONE, DOUBLE BASS, GRAND PIANO, CLARINET, GUITAR, OR BANJO.

- SYNCOPATION: RHYTHMS SHIFT OR CHANGE IN AN UNEXPECTED WAY, FROM THE STRONG BEAT TO THE WEAK BEAT, SO JAZZ MUSIC SOUNDS SURPRISING.

- JAZZ IS NOT COMMONLY SUNG, BUT PLAYED ON INSTRUMENTS.

TROMBONE

Louis wondered what it would be like to play a real horn. A used cornet, an instrument similar to a trumpet, was in a pawnshop window. It cost five dollars. That was so much money. Much more than he made at his job with the Karnofskys. But the Karnofskys were kind. They loaned him money. It took Louis weeks to pay them back but it was worth it. The cornet was dirty and a little beat-up. But Louis loved it. He taught himself the basic notes and practiced all the time.

When he was about ten, Louis and three other boys formed a street singers group. Walking through Storyville, they sang all different kinds of songs. If someone asked for a song, the boys would sing it for them. When they were done, they collected money in a hat. Sometimes, they danced, too, using the kind of steps and movements now called break dancing. Break dancing uses different body movements, spins, arm movements, leg movements, and freezing poses, all of which are done to the rhythm of hip-hop music.

One New Year's Eve, when he was about twelve, Louis and his friends were out singing. Louis brought along a pis-tol someone had left at his mother's place. One of the boys shot off a cap gun. But Louis shot off his real gun. He didn't want to hurt any-

one, but it was a very dangerous thing to do.

COLORED WAIFS' HOME

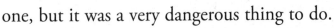

A policeman on duty that night heard the noise. He grabbed Louis from behind. Louis's friends all ran away. Louis cried and begged the policeman to let him go. But he wouldn't; the policeman was as strict as Grandma Josephine. Louis was taken to Juvenile Court and charged with firing a gun in a public place. The judge was strict, too. He sent Louis to live at the Colored Waifs' Home for Boys.

Chapter 2
A Home Away from Home

The Colored Waifs' Home for Boys was only about five miles from Louis's home. It was not far from New Orleans. But to Louis, it must have seemed like being in the country. The grounds were filled with honeysuckle vines, and in the summer, the air was sweet with the perfume of the honeysuckle flowers. For the rest of his life, Louis loved the smell of honeysuckle, and said it was his favorite flower.

The boys in the home worked hard to make it a clean, tidy place to live. Louis learned how to wash and iron clothes, scrub the floors, make his bed,

HONEYSUCKLE

and cook a meal. He also learned to play sports. Best of all, he learned music, although not right away.

At first, Louis was homesick. The Home didn't serve the red beans and rice he liked, only white beans, without rice. For three days he didn't eat. But finally, Louis was too hungry. He ate three bowls of white beans and never missed a meal again.

All the boys and the men who watched over them were Black. Professor Peter Davis taught music. He didn't like Louis at first. He thought Louis was a bad boy from a bad neighborhood. The band was led by Professor Davis. And

joining it was a reward for good behavior. So for six months, Louis followed all the rules of the Home. Finally, Professor Davis invited him to join the band.

TAMBOURINE

Professor Davis first gave Louis a tambourine. Louis was so good with it that, soon, he was promoted to the drums. Then Professor Davis gave him an alto horn and a bugle. Louis learned to play them both. Professor Davis was impressed. He saw Louis's talent and wanted to encourage it.

ALTO HORN

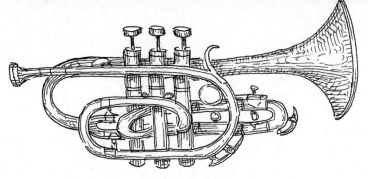

CORNET

Finally, he gave the boy a cornet. Louis was so happy. He could remember musical phrases, and he was quick at picking up a tune. Now, he would learn to play like a pro. Professor Davis showed Louis how to place his mouth on the instrument. He showed his eager pupil how to blow a clear, firm note. Louis learned to play music written by famous European composers from long ago— Franz Liszt, Johann Sebastian Bach, and Gustav Mahler. Soon, Louis was so good that Professor Davis made him leader of the band.

Although the boys in the Home were not allowed to leave, the band could march and play in city parades. In a uniform and cream-colored cap,

Louis marched through his old neighborhood. He was so proud to be the bandleader. His mother and his old friends lined the streets to see the band pass by. They were proud too. Usually, the boys were given peppermint candy and gingerbread cakes as rewards for playing. But this time, the crowd took up a collection, filling several hats with money. The money paid for new uniforms and new instruments. Later, Louis wrote of these years: "My whole [musical] success goes back to

the time I was arrested . . . Because then I had to quit running around and began to learn something. Most of all, I began to learn music."

The judge did not say how long Louis had to stay at the Home for Boys. What Louis needed was an important white person to speak up for him. To say he had changed.

Louis rarely saw his father. But by the time Louis was fourteen, his father had become a supervisor in a turpentine plant. This was a high-ranking job for a Black person at the time. Willie Armstrong asked his boss to appeal for Louis's release. The boss did. And the judge finally agreed to place Louis in his father's care.

On June 16, 1914, Louis left the Home for Boys for good.

Chapter 3
Making Music

Louis lived with his father, stepmother, and stepbrothers for a while. All the things he had learned at the Home for Boys were a help. He could keep the place clean and cook the meals. But after Gertrude, his stepmother, gave birth to her third child, Louis went back to his mother's home.

Louis, now fourteen, was finished with school. He had gone as far as the fifth grade, not counting the classes at the Home for Boys. He was almost grown, and he was ready to support himself. He hauled coal and delivered milk for the Cloverdale Milk Company. Then one day he fell off the wagon. The wagon kept right on going. A wheel ran over his foot and injured it.

Louis had to find a new job. He was, at different times, a dishwasher, house wrecker, and construction worker. For a while he worked unloading bananas from a boat, until a big rat jumped out of a bunch that he was carrying. He dropped the bunch and never ate a banana again.

But whatever he did during the day, Louis found a way to play music at night. At first, he hung out in honky-tonks—cheap dance halls— where he would hold the instruments for the musicians during their breaks. Soon, they began asking Louis to play with them. The owners of the honky-tonks didn't care if the musicians were good. All they wanted were musicians who were willing to play all night for low wages.

But Louis *was* good. In the honky-tonk bars, Louis played in a trio: cornet, piano, and drums. That led to a steady job at a honky-tonk owned by

a man named Ponce. Louis played most of the night, went home to sleep for two hours, and then was off to work again the next day. Mayann packed his meals, so he wouldn't have to spend his money on food.

Louis became a really good cornet player. People took notice of him and the special way that he played his music. In a book that he wrote about his life, he explained it like this: "When a . . . player . . . 'feels' the music taking hold of him so strong . . . he can [take the] . . . rhythms and toss them around as he wants without losing his way."

Soon, his old hero, Joe Oliver, took an interest in him. Joe invited him to dinner and introduced him to Stella, his wife. He gave Louis pointers about fingering—the way to put his fingers on the keys of the cornet. He also gave him a cornet. In return, Louis was happy to do all kinds of chores and errands for Joe and Stella. He called the older man Papa Joe, and said later, "I can never stop loving Joe Oliver."

Then on April 6, 1917, something happened that changed the future of Louis's life and the lives of many of the other jazz musicians in New Orleans. The United States entered World War I, and along with France and England, fought against Germany. Many U.S. sailors were in New Orleans.

WORLD WAR I

WORLD WAR I, OR THE FIRST WORLD
WAR, WAS THE FIRST WAR THAT INVOLVED
COUNTRIES SPANNING MORE THAN HALF
THE GLOBE. IT LASTED FROM 1914 TO 1918
AND WAS ALSO CALLED THE GREAT WAR.
ON ONE SIDE WERE GERMANY, AUSTRIA-
HUNGARY, BULGARIA, AND TURKEY. THEY
WERE CALLED THE CENTRAL POWERS. ON
THE OTHER SIDE WERE FRANCE, ENGLAND,
ITALY, RUSSIA, AND, EVENTUALLY, THE
UNITED STATES—THE ALLIES. THE ALLIES
WON THE WAR.

New Orleans was a large port city and had the room to train and house sailors. Like sailors everywhere, the boys in New Orleans wanted to explore the city's nightlife. They went to bars, honky-tonks, and music joints. One night, some of the sailors were murdered.

The government decided to close Storyville down. The bars, the restaurants, the hotels, and the honky-tonks were now seen as a threat to United States servicemen. But what about all the musicians who played in those places?

Many of them left town, looking for other places to work. Even Joe Oliver packed his bags and went to Chicago. Louis was at the train station to say good-bye. He said it was a ". . . sad parting . . . I felt the old gang was breaking up." But then he found out that he had been chosen to replace Joe Oliver in Kid Ory's band. Oliver himself had suggested it. "What a thrill that was!" Louis said. "To think I was considered up to taking Joe Oliver's place in the best band in town! I couldn't hardly wait to get to Mayann's place to tell her the good news."

By this time, Louis was married to a woman named Daisy Parker. They lived in their own place, a two-room second-floor apartment with a balcony. Louis was now leading the life of a New Orleans jazz musician. He knew every song Kid Ory's band played. He fit right in. While a member of Kid Ory's band, Louis worked out a little dance routine to perform between songs. He described it as a "a little tap dancing and a little fooling around between the numbers to get laughs."

It was during this time that he wrote and sold some songs. "I Wish I Could Shimmy Like My Sister Kate" was one of his earliest hits. Louis sold the rights to it for fifty dollars. The men who bought it—Clarence Williams and Armand Piron—made a fortune on it because it became so popular.

A man named Fate Marable heard Louis play. Marable worked for the Streckfus Steamboat Line and chose bands to play for the passengers. He had

STEAMBOATS & JAZZ

IN THE MID-1800S, STEAMBOATS HAULED FREIGHT UP AND DOWN THE RIVERS AND CANALS THAT CONNECTED THEM. BUT AFTER RAILROADS CONNECTED THE COUNTRY, RIVERBOATS NO LONGER WERE THE ONLY MEANS OF CARRYING GOODS. OVER TIME, RIVERBOATS WERE USED, MORE AND MORE, FOR PLEASURE TRIPS. THEY TOOK PEOPLE FOR SHORT TRIPS UP THE RIVER. FOOD AND DRINKS WERE SERVED. A BAND PLAYED MUSIC FOR DANCING. IN THE WARMER MONTHS, THE BOATS MADE LONGER TRIPS. THEY WOULD STOP AT EACH PORT ALONG THE WAY, PLAYING MUSIC TO ATTRACT CROWDS.

been looking to hire some young Black musicians in New Orleans who were creating the hot, new jazz sound. When he heard Louis, he knew he wanted to hire him.

Louis began performing on boats that took day trips from the port of New Orleans. Then in 1920, he began to play on the steamer *Dixie Belle*, which took longer trips up the Mississippi River. During the trips, he had time on his hands. He learned to read music. Before this, his natural talent allowed him to learn songs and tunes simply by hearing them. Now, he learned to read the actual musical notes that were printed on the score.

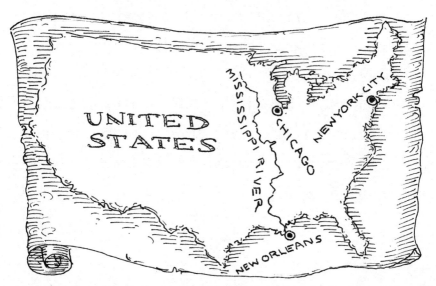

At that time, there was no other Black orchestra going up and down the Mississippi River. In lots of places where they stopped, white people made rude and nasty comments. The band members just kept to themselves. When they started to play, the white people usually quieted down and could appreciate the music they heard.

Louis was soon in demand. In 1921 a bandleader asked Louis to join his band in New York. Some musicians who left New Orleans became famous and successful up North. But others found only poverty and trouble. They came home, worn out and poor. Louis decided he wasn't ready to leave New Orleans. Not yet. Instead, he played with the Tuxedo Brass Band, the best marching band in town.

Papa Joe Oliver hadn't forgotten about Louis, either. He kept writing from Chicago, urging Louis to join him. Finally, in 1922, Louis felt bold enough to try it.

To get ready, he packed his typewriter, his phonograph records, his cornet, and the few clothes he owned. He wore his long underwear, because Mayann didn't want him to get cold. She also packed him a fish sandwich to eat on the train, because Black passengers weren't allowed in the dining car. Louis Armstrong was on his way to Chicago, on his way to the big time.

THE GREAT MIGRATION

IN 1910 OVER 80 PERCENT OF BLACK AMERICANS LIVED IN THE RURAL SOUTH. MOST WORKED IN THE FIELDS, PICKING COTTON. BUT BLACK PEOPLE WERE TIRED OF LIVING UNDER JIM CROW LAWS. AND THERE WERE BETTER JOBS IN THE CITIES UP NORTH.

A GREAT MIGRATION BEGAN, AND THOUSANDS UPON THOUSANDS OF FAMILIES PICKED UP AND MOVED NORTH. DURING WORLD WAR I, BLACK PEOPLE FILLED JOBS HELD BY THE HUNDREDS OF THOUSANDS OF WHITE PEOPLE WHO WERE IN THE MILITARY. SOME EMPLOYERS SENT RECRUITERS SOUTH, BUT MANY BLACK PEOPLE LEARNED ABOUT JOBS FROM NEWSPAPERS, LIKE THE *CHICAGO DEFENDER*.

THE GREAT MIGRATION CONTINUED THROUGH THE 1920S AND 1930S. MOST BLACK PEOPLE TRAVELED NORTH BY TRAIN, TAKING THE CHEAPEST AND MOST DIRECT ROUTE. BLACK PEOPLE FROM SOUTH CAROLINA, NORTH CAROLINA, AND VIRGINIA MOST OFTEN WENT TO NEW YORK, PHILADELPHIA, AND BOSTON. BLACK PEOPLE FROM GEORGIA AND ALABAMA OFTEN MOVED TO CLEVELAND, PITTSBURGH, AND DETROIT. BLACK PEOPLE FROM MISSISSIPPI AND LOUISIANA MOST OFTEN MOVED TO CHICAGO. BY 1970, ONLY ABOUT 25 PERCENT OF BLACK PEOPLE LIVED IN THE RURAL SOUTH.

Chapter 4
King of Jazz

When Louis Armstrong arrived in Chicago, Papa Joe wasn't there to meet his train. Louis had arrived later than planned. He had stayed in New Orleans to play in a funeral and earn some spending money for his trip.

Funerals in New Orleans were filled with music. Bands followed the casket to the cemetery and played sad music. But on the way back, they played happy, joyful music to remind everyone that life went on.

Louis stood waiting at the railroad station for Papa Joe. After an hour-and-a-half, Louis felt brave enough to ask for help. It turned out that Papa Joe had been there and left. So now, Louis made his way to the Lincoln Gardens, on

Chicago's South Side. That's where Joe Oliver's Creole Jazz Band was performing. He listened to them play and met the band members. He knew Oliver was great, but Louis heard people calling Papa Joe "King Oliver."

Joe Oliver took Louis to a boardinghouse on South Wabash Avenue. It was the first time Louis had ever lived in a place with indoor plumbing. Back in New Orleans, there was only an outhouse and a tin tub for bathing.

Louis became a cornetist in King Oliver's band. The band was a big success. Joe and Louis played duets that they seemed to improvise—or make

up—on the spot. Actually, a few minutes before they started, Oliver played the tune he planned to use. Then he and Armstrong just took off, inventing new variations on the music. Each time they played, it was a little bit different. Armstrong's deep chest and strong lips helped him out. He could blow long and hard on any brass horn, and the sound was always pure and true. Years later, Louis Armstrong said, ". . . They called me 'Iron Lips' Armstrong or 'Brass Lips' because I could blow more high C notes in succession than any swing trumpeter in the world . . . . I like to get way up there and hold onto that clear high note."

A new piano player joined the band. Her name was Lil Hardin. Lil had gone to college in Tennessee and had been trained in classical music. Still, she liked playing jazz better. She thought that Louis wore awful clothes and that his haircut was even worse. Louis thought that a college graduate would never be interested in him. But they fell in love, anyway. Louis divorced Daisy, and in 1924 he married Lil.

Lil was a big believer in Louis Armstrong's talent. She thought he was even better than Papa Joe. She told him that if he stayed in Oliver's band, he would never be the lead player. Lil thought that Louis should leave Chicago, even if she had to stay behind. This time, when the New York bandleader asked him to come to New York, Louis said yes.

Louis was now twenty-three years old. He performed with the band at the famous Roseland Ballroom at Broadway and Fifty-First Street in New York City. It was the first Black band to perform there. The people who came to Roseland were mostly white, and they came to dance.

BESSIE SMITH

Besides playing at Roseland, Louis also played at after-hours clubs in Harlem in Manhattan. Harlem was a famous Black neighborhood that was home to many jazz clubs. He recorded his music with popular jazz and blues stars like singers Bessie Smith and Ma Rainey. The recordings were called "race records" and had an almost all-Black audience.

But playing at Roseland wasn't everything Louis Armstrong dreamed of. Many of his fellow band members didn't take the music seriously enough. They came onstage drunk.

MA RAINEY

HARLEM IN MANHATTAN

BLACK MUSICIANS IN JAZZ AND BLUES

THERE WERE MANY BLACK MUSICIANS WHO CONTRIBUTED TO THE GROWTH OF JAZZ. THEY WERE BANDLEADERS, LIKE DUKE ELLINGTON, WHO WAS A CONDUCTOR AND COMPOSER. COUNT BASIE WAS ANOTHER FAMOUS BANDLEADER WITH HIS OWN ORCHESTRA. PIANO PLAYER FLETCHER HENDERSON AND SAXOPHONE PLAYER DON REDMAN PLAYED IN THE BIG BANDS POPULAR FROM THE 1920S TO THE 1940S. CHARLIE PARKER WAS ANOTHER FAMOUS SAXOPHONIST, LOVED FOR HIS ORIGINALITY AND THE LIGHTNING SPEED WITH WHICH HE PLAYED.

JAZZ IS MOSTLY INSTRUMENTAL MUSIC—MUSIC PLAYED ON INSTRUMENTS, NOT SUNG. BUT JAZZ ALSO INFLUENCED MANY SINGERS, WHO SANG IN A JAZZ STYLE. SOME OF THE MOST FAMOUS WERE ELLA FITZGERALD, BILLIE HOLIDAY, AND SARAH VAUGHAN—ALL BLACK SINGERS. ELLA FITZGERALD ALSO RECORDED SOME SONGS WITH LOUIS ARMSTRONG LATER ON IN HIS CAREER.

DUKE ELLINGTON

After about a year in New York, Louis had had enough. He went back to Chicago, where Lil was waiting.

Lil managed Louis's career. She was performing at Bill Bottoms' Dreamland Café and got her husband there for seventy-five dollars a week. Back then, a ride on the bus cost five cents. A meal in a restaurant might cost a quarter. Seventy-five dollars was a lot of money.

Together, Louis and Lil bought a house in the South Side of Chicago. The area was called Bronzeville or the Black Belt, because so many Black people lived there. The Armstrongs also bought a car and some land by Lake Idlewild in Michigan.

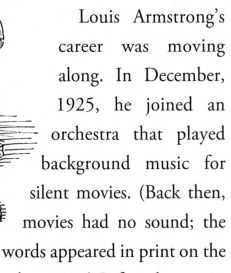

Louis Armstrong's career was moving along. In December, 1925, he joined an orchestra that played background music for silent movies. (Back then, movies had no sound; the words appeared in print on the screen in between the scenes.) Before the movie, the band played, and during breaks, the band members each played some solos.

The brass or horn section was led by Jimmy Tate. He needed another trumpet, not a cornet, and so he asked Louis to switch instruments. Louis had been a little afraid of the trumpet before. He thought it was a "fancy" instrument that belonged in a classical orchestra. But once he got used to it, he never went back. He played trumpet for the rest of his life.

POPULAR JAZZ TERMS

JAZZ MUSICIANS HAD THEIR OWN SPECIAL WAY OF TALKING. HERE ARE SOME OF THE WORDS THEY USED AND WHAT THEY MEANT BY THEM:

BALLAD: SLOW SONG OR MUSICAL COMPOSITION

BEBOP: A STYLE OF JAZZ THAT HAS A JAGGED BEAT

BLUES: A STYLE OF MUSIC THAT GREW UP ALONG WITH JAZZ; SONGS ARE ABOUT HARD LUCK AND BAD TIMES

CAT: MUSICIAN

COOL JAZZ: A FLUID STYLE POPULAR IN THE 1940S AND EARLY 1950S

FRETS: RIDGES ON THE KEYBOARD OF A STRINGED INSTRUMENT, LIKE A GUITAR OR BANJO

RAGTIME: PIANO MUSIC MARKED BY SYNCOPATED OR "JUMPING" RHYTHM

GIG: JOB

RIFFS: SINGLE RHYTHMIC PHRASES REPEATED OVER AGAIN IN JAZZ AND BLUES MUSIC

SCATTING: SINGING MADE-UP, NONSENSE SOUNDS INSTEAD OF WORDS IN A SONG

SOUL-JAZZ: A STYLE INFLUENCED BY GOSPEL OR CHURCH MUSIC

SWING: A STYLE OF JAZZ THAT HAS A FLUID, EASY RHYTHM

In 1926 Louis joined the Carroll Dickerson Band at the Sunset Cafe. The sign, spelled out in lights, said: *LOUIS ARMSTRONG, WORLD'S GREATEST TRUMPET PLAYER*. Later, he wrote, "I will never forget the kick I got when I first saw that bright sign." It was clear: Louis Armstrong was now the King of Jazz.

White musicians heard about him and came to hear him play. They hoped to learn a few of his tricks. By 1926, he also started to sing on some of his own recordings. He had a rough, gravelly voice that added to the moody sound he was trying to create. People—both Black and white—loved it.

One time, Louis was recording one of his own hit songs, "Heebie Jeebies." Back then, a musician had to record the whole piece straight through. If he made a mistake, he could not stop and start again. Armstrong said that during the recording session, he dropped the sheet music. He had to keep singing, even though he didn't have the words to look at. So he sang silly, nonsense syllables instead of the actual words to the song. Words like these: "Boo bop, bee bop, boppy, booby, boo." It was a mistake. But people liked the way it sounded.

This kind of music is known as scat singing. Some musicians say that Armstrong invented it. Scat became very popular with other singers. Jazz musicians started to copy the sound and still use it today. The famous singer and movie star Bing Crosby listened to Louis Armstrong's scat recordings and used scat singing on his own records.

BING CROSBY

In 1927 Louis's mother, Mayann, came to visit him in Chicago. It turned out to be her last visit. She died in her son's house, and he was able to give her a large, expensive funeral. "Her funeral in Chicago is probably the only time I ever cried," he said later.

Still, he went on playing and recording his music. At that time, Black performers were expected to entertain the audience by acting silly onstage. Louis understood this and went along with the routine. Making funny faces, rolling his eyes, and goofing around, he made the audience—both Black and white—feel relaxed and comfortable. But underneath his pranks, he was dead serious about the music. The music always came first.

Because of money troubles, Louis wrote an exercise book called *Louis Armstrong's 50 Hot Choruses for Cornet.* Even though he now played the trumpet, the cornet had been his first instrument, so he knew a lot about it. He had used books like the one he wrote when he was younger.

In 1929 Louis's band left Chicago for New York City. With money from the sales of his book, Louis bought a new car and drove east, stopping at Niagara Falls in upstate New York and at other tourist spots. He liked the

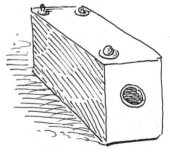

EASTMAN KODAK
BOX CAMERA

NIAGARA FALLS

new box cameras that the Kodak company had recently made popular. For the rest of his life, Armstrong took pictures of himself and his friends.

Eventually, the band reached New York City, where they were scheduled to play at clubs in Harlem, and on one of the world's most famous streets: Broadway.

Chapter 5
Ups and Downs

Louis Armstrong had once tried managing his own band. He found he didn't like the job. He liked playing his music. Let someone else work out all the details of where and when the band played. Louis chose a man named Tommy Rockwell to be his manager. Tommy Rockwell wanted Louis Armstrong to be a soloist. He was such a great musician, he didn't need a band, Rockwell said. When Louis and his band arrived in New York, Rockwell was angry. He had work for Louis, not for the others. Still, Louis wouldn't fire them. Instead, he found them work at a Black music hall called the Audubon.

Then Rockwell got Louis a job performing in a show called *Hot Chocolates* in Harlem. It was a huge success. The music was by Fats Waller. Louis sang a song called "Ain't Misbehavin'" and the audience went wild. It became one of his most popular songs and is still a jazz classic. *Hot Chocolates* was so successful that

FATS WALLER

it moved to Broadway's Hudson Theater.

All through the 1930s, Louis Armstrong did a lot of touring throughout the rest of the country. By now, America was deep in the Great Depression. The stock market crash of 1929 had destroyed the economy. Millions of people lost their jobs, their homes, and their savings.

Music helped cheer people up. It took their minds off their troubles.

BIG BANDS VS. JAZZ BANDS

FROM THE 1920S TO THE 1940S, BIG BANDS WERE POPULAR IN THE UNITED STATES. WHILE JAZZ BANDS WERE SMALL (MAYBE TEN MUSICIANS), BIG BANDS WERE . . . BIG! THERE WERE USUALLY AROUND TWENTY MUSICIANS, AND OFTEN A LEAD SINGER. BIG BANDS PLAYED SET MUSICAL PIECES. THEY DIDN'T IMPROVISE THE WAY JAZZ MUSICIANS DID. PART OF THE REASON FOR THIS WAS THE RISE OF RECORD COMPANIES AND RADIO SHOWS. A SONG COULD NOT BE A DIFFERENT LENGTH EACH TIME IT WAS PLAYED; IT HAD TO FIT INTO A FIXED TIME SLOT. BIG BANDS BEGAN TO DIE OUT AFTER WORLD WAR II WAS OVER.

HOLLYWOOD

Now big bands were popular, and Armstrong was often the featured soloist. During one trip, Louis went out to Hollywood, California, where movies were made and movie stars lived. He had learned how to dress better by this time and wore an ascot tie with an extra big knot. Soon, lots of men were copying him and wearing "Louis Armstrong knots."

Louis Armstrong stayed in Hollywood for about a year, making records and appearing on radio

shows. Sound films were replac-
ing the silent films of the 1920s.
Directors were looking for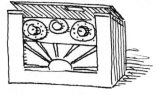
people with interesting or unusual voices. Louis's
rough, sandpapery voice was just the thing.

At that time, there were limited roles for Black
actors in the movies. Black people had to
play servants or faithful companions. A Black man
couldn't be a star in his own right. When Louis
was in a film, parts were written just for him, to
show off his singing and trumpet-playing. The
parts also took advantage of his natural comic
gifts, and his bubbly personality. Louis liked to

entertain people. So he accepted the roles and played them well, even though the dialogue was often silly. Years later, some people criticized Louis for taking these parts. They said that the parts made Black people look foolish.

Louis returned to Chicago in 1931. His relationship with Lil was in trouble. Neither of them was happy. They soon divorced.

Back on the road, Armstrong found a new manager, a white man named Johnny Collins. He also hired a white bus driver. Black bands needed to have white men for protection. Otherwise, a busload of Black people might be treated badly or even thrown into jail.

Louis's band traveled and performed throughout the South. This was not an easy thing to do at that time. When the band arrived in a new town, the men could not check into a white hotel. Instead, they had to find a place in the Black part of town. It was the same with restaurants. Some places wouldn't serve Black people. Other places had "whites only" bathrooms. Louis and the band suffered a lot of insults.

But when Louis Armstrong paid a visit to his hometown, New Orleans, he received a hero's wel-

come. Waiting to greet him at the train station were brass bands. There was a huge crowd of both Black and white people. His fans paraded around him through the city streets.

Louis was so popular, a cigar was named after him. It was called the Louis Armstrong Special.

A local baseball team changed its name to Armstrong's Secret Nine. Louis agreed to become

the team's sponsor. He supplied the money for the team uniforms.

The band was going to play many concerts at the Suburban Gardens. When the first concert began, Louis's friends and neighbors could not attend because

ARMSTRONG'S SECRET NINE.

the hall was filled with white people. The Black people had to stand outside. If they were lucky, they got to hear the music through the open windows.

The concerts were also going to be broadcast

on the radio. On the first night, the white radio announcer refused to introduce a Black band on the air. He marched off the stage. What would happen now? Louis Armstrong stepped in. He asked the band to play a long chord while he walked onstage. Everyone clapped and cheered. Louis quieted the crowd and then started the show. The announcer who walked off was fired.

For the next three months, Louis did all his own announcing. He wanted to do a special concert for all the Black people before leaving New Orleans. But when he showed up to play, he found that the police had sent everyone home. Over and over, Louis saw how racist white people couldn't accept Black musicians, even brilliant and talented ones.

Louis went to play at the Royal Theater in Baltimore, Maryland. The theater was in a poor neighborhood. Many people didn't even have money to buy coal to heat their houses. Louis stopped at a coal yard and ordered a ton—that's two thousand pounds—of coal. He asked that it be delivered to the lobby of the Royal Theater. People—Black or white—who needed coal could come and help themselves.

In 1932 Louis took his first trip to England. When he got there, his nickname of Satchelmouth got shortened. From then on, he became known as

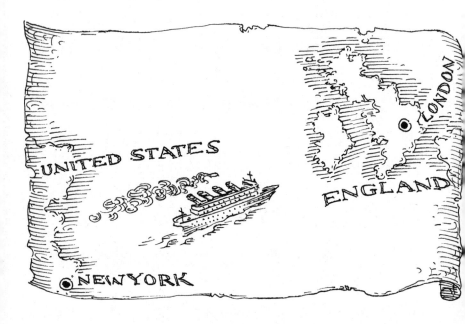

Satchmo. Louis played to packed halls in England, too. He used his trademark white handkerchief to

wipe his face and give signals to the band.

When he returned to the United States in November, his lip was sore. He needed to take time off from playing. But Collins continued to get him jobs. Collins also drank too much, and kept Louis's money.

The lip got worse. Louis had to stop playing until it healed. During this time, Louis realized that Collins was not paying bills or sending money to Lil. So Louis fired Collins and then took a long vacation in 1934. While he rested his lip, he visited Paris, France, a city without the kind of prejudice that existed in the United States.

In January, 1935, he returned

EIFFEL TOWER

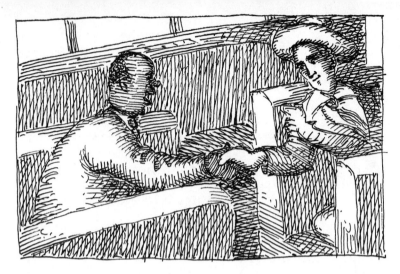

home. This time, he chose an old friend, Joe Glaser, as his manager. Glaser used to run the Sunset Cafe in Chicago. They remained together for the rest of Louis Armstrong's life. Unlike many white people at the time, Glaser traveled on the bus *with* Louis and the band, not in a separate car.

Once his lip was better, Armstrong was eager to start playing and performing again. A magazine interview quoted him as saying, "My chops is fine now . . . and I'm dying to swing out again. They gave me a new trumpet over in Europe, and I've got a smaller mouthpiece than I had on my old horn . . . . I'm all rested up and dying to get going again."

There was something else he was dying to do, as

well. From the very first time he left New Orleans, Satchmo had taken along a typewriter. He liked to write about his childhood, his start in music, his travels, the people he met, and the music he played. In 1936 his first book, *Swing That Music*,

SWING THAT MUSIC

BY LOUIS ARMSTRONG

was published. It was the very first autobiography written by a jazz musician.

The year 1937 was another first for Louis Armstrong. He stood in for his friend, the white movie star Rudy Vallee, on a popular radio show. It was the first time a Black person hosted a national radio program, and it opened the door for other Black performers all over the country.

Louis Armstrong sang a song called "Jeepers Creepers" to a horse in

RUDY VALLEE

the 1938 movie *Going Places*. In the film, the horse was wild and out of control until

Louis sang to him. Then the horse grew calm and cooperative. Louis earned an Academy Award nomination for his performance.

Chapter 6
A Question of Color

In December, 1941, the United States entered World War II. Soldiers fought in Europe against Germany and Italy, and in the South Pacific against Japan. Louis Armstrong went overseas to entertain American soldiers. Playing at military bases in Europe and Asia, he helped bring the sound of jazz across the Atlantic and Pacific Oceans.

In 1942 Louis married again. Lucille Wilson was the perfect wife for him. Though she had been trained in music, she was not a musician. Instead, she devoted herself to making her husband happy. When Louis returned to New York City from a tour in 1943, Lucille told him to meet her at 34-56 107th Street in Corona, a neighborhood in Queens. He arrived there, but didn't see her. So he

ARMSTRONG HOUSE QUEENS, N.Y.

knocked on the door. Lucille opened it and said, "Welcome home, honey."

The house was completely furnished. There was a hot meal waiting for him. The house in Corona was exactly the home Louis had always wanted. Lucille and Louis lived there for the rest of his life.

The war ended in 1945. So did the popularity of big bands. Louis tried a small band called Louis Armstrong and His All Stars. Some of the musi-

THE ALL STARS

INTEGRATED JAM SESSION
PARAMOUNT THEATER, NEW YORK

cians were Black and some were white. Long before segregation came to an end, Armstrong was working with an integrated band—Black and white people playing together. He knew that skin color did not count. What mattered was the music, and how well you could play it. The All Stars played all over the United States and Europe, too.

In 1949 *TIME* magazine featured a photograph of Louis Armstrong on the cover of its February 21 issue. It pictured him as the King of Jazz, wearing a hand-drawn crown of cornets, his first instrument. He was also crowned king of the Mardi Gras in his hometown of New Orleans. The mayor gave him the keys to the city. He was welcomed as a local hero.

During the 1950s, Louis Armstrong kept performing with his All Stars. Even though rock

and roll became the new musical craze, people still wanted to listen to Armstrong.

The country was changing in other ways, too. The Civil Rights Movement began to challenge the old laws. Black people wanted equal housing, schools, and job opportunities. Slowly, life for Black people, especially in the South, began to change.

Many Black people felt that Louis had betrayed them—he hadn't been active enough in the struggle for equality. They even called him Uncle Tom, after a character in a famous nineteenth century

novel, *Uncle Tom's Cabin*. In the book, Uncle Tom never stands up to his white owner, but tries instead to please him by obeying.

Calling a Black person an Uncle Tom was an insult. And Louis Armstrong was hurt and surprised. "How can they say that?" he wrote. "I've pioneered in breaking the color lines in many Southern states . . . . I've taken a lot of abuse, put up with a lot of jazz, even been in some pretty dangerous spots through no fault of my own for almost forty years."

He and Lucille traveled to Africa for the first time in 1956. Louis wanted to visit the land of his ancestors, in the colony of Gold Coast. (It is now

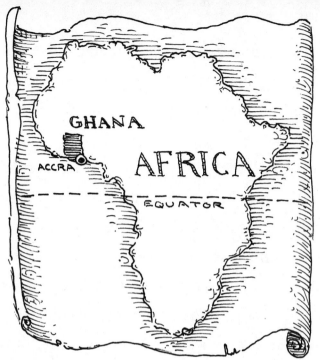

the country of Ghana.) Fans met him at the airport. Ghanaian men carried him by hand in a sedan chair, as was their custom. More than one

hundred thousand people attended his concert. Armstrong appreciated the warm welcome. It helped him forget about the insults in the United States.

In 1957 the governor of Arkansas tried to stop the first Black students from attending an all-white school. Louis Armstrong spoke out now. He made his first public statement about race and civil rights. "It's getting so bad, a colored man hasn't got any country," he told a reporter. And he added that the governor of Arkansas was an "uneducated plow boy." Louis Armstrong was standing up to racism in his own way.

Chapter 7
Hello and Good-bye

All during the 1950s and 1960s, Armstrong kept playing and recording his music, though many people felt his most original music and most creative years were behind him. He also kept touring, giving concerts in Nigeria, Central Africa, Ghana, and Kenya. He even went to segregated countries, like Rhodesia, a British colony that is now Zimbabwe and Zambia.

In 1963 he recorded the popular song "Hello, Dolly!" By 1964, it was a smash hit, even more

popular than the Beatles' song "She Loves You." Louis Armstrong was on the cover of the April 15, 1966 issue of *LIFE* magazine. His 1967 song "What a Wonderful World" also became a hit all over the world.

Unfortunately, Louis Armstrong's health was failing. In September of 1968, he had a bad heart attack. When he left the hospital, he was still weak. The death of his longtime manager, Joe Glaser, hit him hard, too.

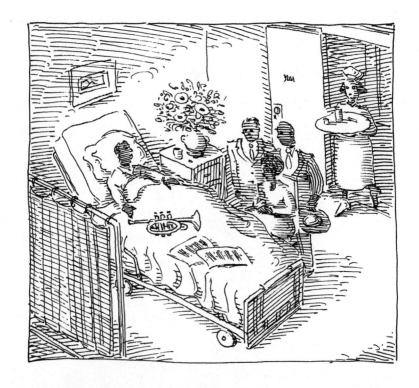

LOUIS AND BARBRA

The last movie that Louis made was *Hello, Dolly!*, which came out in 1969. In it, he appeared with singer-actress Barbra Streisand. Soon after, he was set to play at the Waldorf Astoria Hotel in New York City for two weeks. His doctors warned against it. Here is what Louis said: "Doc, you don't understand. My whole life, my whole soul, my whole spirit is to blow that horn. I've got to do it." He played at the Waldorf, even though it wore

him out. Afterward, he checked into a hospital for two months. On July 5, he was planning to start rehearsing for another tour. But the very next day, July 6, 1971, Louis Armstrong died quietly in his sleep with Lucille by his side.

During his life, Louis Armstrong had a full and rich career. He recorded hit songs for nearly fifty years and his music is still heard today on the radio, on television, and in movies. Although he never went to high school, he wrote two autobiographies, over ten magazine articles, and hundreds of pages of memoirs and thousands of letters. He composed dozens of songs that have become jazz classics, and he performed an average of three hundred concerts a year, all over the world. He was also a gifted actor and appeared in over thirty films.

When he died, Louis Armstrong was hailed as a musical hero. President Richard Nixon called him "a free and individual spirit, and an artist of worldwide fame." The president arranged for

Louis Armstrong's body to lie in state at the Seventh Regiment Armory at Park Avenue and 66th Street in New York City. Twenty-five thousand people came to pay their last respects.

The joy Louis Armstrong felt in playing his trumpet was strong, constant, and unmistakable. He shared that joy with listeners. His spirit lives on, through jazz musicians who came after him, and through the beautiful music he created.

TIMELINE OF LOUIS ARMSTRONG'S LIFE

1901	Louis Armstrong born in New Orleans, Louisiana
1903	Beatrice, Louis's sister is born
1913	Sent to Colored Waifs' Home for Boys
1914	Begins musical career
1916	Meets Joe Oliver
1918	Replaces Oliver in Kid Ory's band; marries Daisy Parker
1919	Works on riverboats for Fate Marable
1922	Goes to Chicago to play with Joe Oliver's Creole Jazz Band
1923	Makes first records
1924	Marries Lillian Hardin; goes to New York City
1925	Returns to Chicago. First plays trumpet
1927	Louis's mother, Mayann, dies in Chicago
1929	Stars in *Hot Chocolates* on Broadway; starts playing in big bands
1931	Returns to New Orleans to play
1935	Joe Glaser becomes Louis's manager
1936	Publishes *Swing That Music*, first autobiography
1938	Marries Alpha Smith
1942	Marries Lucille Watson
1943	Moves to Corona, Queens, in New York City
1949	*TIME* magazine article calls him "The King of Jazz"
1954	Publishes *Satchmo, My Life in New Orleans*, second autobiography
1960	Tours Africa
1964	"Hello, Dolly!" becomes a number-one song
1968	"What a Wonderful World" becomes a hit all over the world
1971	Louis Armstrong dies on July 6

Timeline of the World

World War I begins	1914
World War I ends	1918
19th amendment gives women the right to vote	1920
Bubble gum invented	1928
Stock market crashes; Great Depression begins	1929
Franklin Delano Roosevelt elected president	1932
World War II begins in Europe; *The Wizard of Oz* is released in the United States	1939
United States enters World War II	1941
World War II ends	1945
Modern Civil Rights Movement begins when Rosa Parks refuses to give up her seat on a bus in Alabama	1955
Mattel company introduces the first Barbie doll	1959
John F. Kennedy is elected president	1960
More than 250,000 demonstrators march peacefully to the Lincoln Memorial in Washington, D.C., where Martin Luther King Jr. gives his famous "I Have a Dream" speech	1963
The Beatles debut on the *Ed Sullivan Show*	1964
Richard M. Nixon elected president	1968
Neil Armstrong is the first person to walk on the moon	1969
First Earth Day celebrated	1970
26th amendment gives eighteen-year-olds the right to vote	1971

BIBLIOGRAPHY

Not all the facts of Louis Armstrong's life are certain. This was true for many Black people who were born at the turn of the twentieth century. Louis Armstrong did not have his own birth record and was not even sure of the exact date he was born. He found out as much as he could about his early childhood and basically made up the rest. As the years passed, his recollection of events also changed. The books that I relied on most to write this book were:

Bergreen, Laurence. **Louis Armstrong: An Extravagant Life.** Broadway Books, New York, 1997.

Brothers, Thomas, ed., introduction. **Louis Armstrong, In His Own Words.** Oxford University Press, New York, 1999.

Elmer, Howard. **Blues: Its Birth and Growth.** Rosen Publishing Group, New York, 1999.

Hudson, Wade and Valerie Wilson Wesley. **Book of Black Heroes from A to Z: An Introduction to Important Black Achievers.** Just Us Books, New Jersey, 1988.

Lee, Jeanne. **Jam!: The Story of Jazz Music.** Rosen Publishing Group, New York, 1999.

McKissack, Patricia and Frederick. **Louis Armstrong: Jazz Musician.** Enslow Publishers, New Jersey, 1991.

Medearis, Angela Shelf and Michael R. Medearis. **African American Arts: Music.** Henry Holt and Company, New York, 1997.

Miller, Marc H., ed. **Louis Armstrong, A Cultural Legacy.** University of Washington Press, Washington, 1994.

Old, Wendie C. **Louis Armstrong: King of Jazz.** Enslow Publishers, New Jersey, 1998.

Tanenhaus, Sam. **Louis Armstrong, Musician.** Chelsea House Publishers, Pennsylvania, 1989.